II1006742

Presented to

_____

By

_____

On the Occasion of

_____

Date

_____

COME SIT AWHILE

The BLESSINGS OF FAMILY AND HOME

INSPIRATION *from the* FRONT PORCH

by Roy Lessin & Heather Solum

BARBOUR
PUBLISHING

Cover design by Greg Jackson, Jackson Design Co, llc

Cover and interior art by Barbara Pascolini

Published by Barbour Publishing, Inc., P.O. Box 719, Uhrichsville, Ohio 44683, www.barbourbooks.com

Our mission is to publish and distribute inspirational products offering exceptional value and biblical encouragement to the masses.

Member of the
Evangelical Christian
Publishers Association

Printed in China.
5 4 3 2 1

The *Come Sit Awhile* gift book series is a collection of heartwarming stories, scriptures, recipes, quotes, prayers, and inspirational thoughts of hope and encouragement. We have chosen the theme of the front porch because it not only speaks of a place where people gather, relax, and enjoy the pleasures of each other's company, but it is also symbolic of a special place in our hearts where rest is found, where we enjoy the sweetness of God's presence, and where priceless memories are gathered and cherished always.

Jesus answered and said to him,

"If anyone loves Me,

he will keep My word;

and My Father will love him,

and We will come to him

and make Our home with him."

JOHN 14:23 NKJV

There is a place in the heart that is like a front porch. It is a place where we gaze upon a vista of beautiful things, moments, and memories. One of the most cherished views is the flower garden of grace that God has planted around us. The fragrance from this garden comes to us through the loving care of those who are dearest and closest to us. It is the nurturing that we received as children, the guidance that covered us as we grew, and the wisdom that has been imparted to us for a lifetime that allow us to bask in the blessings of family and home.

*Y*OUR HEART CAN HOLD
A JOURNALFUL OF MEMORIES
THAT HAVE BEEN GATHERED
FROM THE TIMES
YOU HAVE SPENT AT HOME.

Things you're likely to find on a porch—

a straw broom,

woven baskets,

potted plants,

crocks,

a porch swing,

rockers,

weatherworn furniture. . .

Other things you're likely to find on a front porch—

books and magazines,

coffee mugs,

reading glasses,

a pitcher of lemonade,

a footstool,

cushions,

a straw hat,

wreath-shaped grapevines. . .

*L*ord, make our home a collection of beautiful things. Make it a gathering place for family and friends—a place where people want to come and be together. Make it a welcoming place for the new acquaintances that are made and for the strangers whom You bring into our lives. Make it a caring place where the needy can find help and the hurting can find comfort. Most of all, make it a loving place where all who enter will sense the sweetness of Your presence.

Be inventive

in hospitality.

ROMANS 12:13 MSG

ospitality is not defined by a large house, fine food, or fancy china. It is defined by the welcoming of the heart, the opening of the home, and the extending of love to every guest.

During hot summer nights
on our farm in Iowa we
enjoyed this cool, refreshing
lemonade treat.

HANNAH KENNEDY

Front Porch Lemonade

Makes 2 ½ quarts

1 cup sugar
9 cups water
1 cup lemon juice
Plenty of ice
Lemon slices for garnish

Combine 1 cup sugar with 1 cup water in a small
saucepan to make a sugar syrup. Bring to boil;
reduce to simmer for five minutes. Remove from
heat and let cool. In large pitcher, combine sugar
syrup, lemon juice, and remaining water. Stir
well. Chill and pour over ice. Serve with lemon
slice and a smile.

Room for Guests

When there is room in the heart,

there is room in the home.

People are often like ferns under the porch in the summertime; they need protective shade in order to thrive.

_____

The LORD *watches over you—*
the LORD *is your shade*
at your right hand.

PSALM 121:5 NIV

My Favorite Porch

The front porch at my mother's house is small and square. It has four steps made of brown bricks leading up to it and a concrete sidewalk that stretches, like a tiny gray highway, through the front yard. The sidewalk is full of wonderful things, like paw prints of animals that couldn't wait till it was dry and the handprints of little children—my brother and me—labeled and dated

in my best first-grade handwriting. A yellow dog named Max sits on the front porch—lounges on it, really—guarding that sacred ground. . . .

The porch is important and special to me because of what it represents—my home, my childhood, my family. It was on that porch where my little friends and I held fashion shows while my mother filmed us. The porch was our stage, the sidewalk our runway; and our audience, other than my mother, was the dog (and any other farm animals that might have happened by). It was there I learned you could cut open a persimmon seed and find tiny silverware inside. It was also the place for shucking corn picked from the garden, pitting cherries from the orchard, or peeling peaches my dad picked out of the tree in the yard. We rarely had callers there. . .only a few unfamiliar visitors who didn't use the back door. It was a thrill to invite a florist, or a prom date, or someone otherwise there on business in from the front porch.

I love to sit on the front porch, as I have so many times throughout the years, with members of my family. I love it at night when the stars above are dancing, like diamonds on a black velvet sea. . .and the bullfrogs are bellowing the blues across the ponds. . . and the whippoorwills are singing their songs to each other in the trees. I love it in the day. . .to feel the country sunshine on my face and smell the flowers that surround the porch—mostly roses and big hydrangeas—and look out into the wide-open field that extends from our front yard. . . .

From the front porch I can see the garden where my grandfather worked and where he once showed me a nest of baby bunnies—where my father gardens now. I can see the trails made by my brother Jim and me as we rode the go-kart through the field, singing and racing the moon home at dusk. There's a now-rickety basketball hoop and a homemade baseball diamond and the place where we dug worms for fishing. I can also see in the distance, where cattle now lie in the shade, a grove of cedars where we played, imagining it to be a mysterious forest. And, if I close my eyes, I can still see us chasing fireflies out in the field at night and bringing them to my parents on the porch to put in jars for safekeeping. . . .

That dear front porch is a humble porch, and in its small square space, it holds my fondest old memories. . .as well as my dreams for new ones to be made. And in my heart, like a gentle whisper I can hear wherever I am, it bids me to sit and rest awhile, and to "Come home."

GWEN FAULKENBERRY

THE SPECIAL MOMENTS
AND CHERISHED MEMORIES
THAT COME FROM
A FRONT PORCH
ARE ALL HOMEMADE.

Aunt Delma's Chicken Salad

Serves 6

2 cups cooked chicken,
   cut into bite-sized pieces

1 cup rosemary pasta, cooked

1 cup celery, cut up into small chunks

1 cup pineapple chunks, drained

½ cup almonds, salted and toasted

½ cup mayonnaise

Olives for garnish (optional)

Sweet pickles for garnish (optional)

Mix together and chill.

Serve in lettuce cups; or cut a whole tomato into flowerlike shape and serve salad in tomato.

Garnish with olives or sweet pickles.

In Minnesota, Aunt Delma's chicken salad was
lovingly shared with family and friends on special
occasions, such as graduation open houses,
Fourth of July picnics, and fiftieth wedding
anniversary celebrations.

GRACE IS AVAILABLE. . .

FOR THE MOTHER WHO

    seeks God's peace in the midst of life's demands;

FOR THE FATHER WHO

    desires to provide the right example;

FOR THE CHILD WHO

    wants to grow in strength of character;

FOR THE FRIEND WHO

    wants to be found faithful;

FOR THE CARING SOULS WHO

    want to touch the lives of others.

A cozy porch is

a great place to

warm up a heart.

In the house of the righteous

is much treasure.

PROVERBS 15:6 KJV

---

*B*y wisdom a house is built,

and through understanding it is established;

through knowledge its rooms are filled

with rare and beautiful treasures.

PROVERBS 24:3–4 NIV

The best
kind of porch
is one with
stories to tell
and memories that linger.

A real treat for children and grandchildren alike, these popcorn balls were especially welcomed when the air was crisp and the leaves turned color in the autumn season.

Grandma Carol's Popcorn Balls

½ cup sugar

½ cup brown sugar

¾ cup dark corn syrup

¼ cup butter

⅔ cup sweetened condensed milk

Approximately 4 quarts popped corn

Combine first five indgredients in a heavy saucepan. Bring to a boil and boil until it reaches soft ball stage, stirring constantly. Let cool. Pour over popcorn; coat well. Form into loose balls.

CAROL SOLUM

Grandpa and Our Great Porch

I fell in love with porches when I was a very young girl. My grandparents had a great porch. They lived in the country, and their porch surrounded two sides of their white two-story house. It was a long porch, and my brother and sisters loved to run up and down the length of it chasing each other. But the best part of the porch was the old metal glider that sat in front of the living room window. It had stuffed cushions that seemed to wrap themselves around you when you sat down. It was there that Grandpa would tell us stories or we would talk about God and His love for us. . . .

I especially liked sitting together with Grandpa on that porch on a hot summer afternoon to watch a thunderstorm come in. It would start with the thunder in the distance, then along would come the gentle breeze that would bring the smell that only comes before the rain. I would jump and get frightened by the clap of thunder, but Grandpa was there to hold me close and tell me about how God made the storm to refresh the earth and clean the air, and how the water allowed our garden to grow and provided water for the well. Somehow, after that, I was no longer afraid and would look forward to the rain and the warmth of my Grandpa's lap. . . .

The porch had a cellar door in its floor. It led to a dark, damp, and musty room located under the house, where I knew scary things were waiting to grab a little girl who would dare to enter it alone. However, this all changed when Grandpa would need to go to the cellar for a jar of peaches or pears that my grandmother had made and ask me to go along. Somehow he was able to bring a special light and warmth to this area that took away all fear and apprehension I may have had when the door was lifted open, and I descended the steps with him.

Grandpa has provided me with many special memories. He was a kind and gentle man. I know he loved me very much, and that is why this porch has such a special place in my heart.

GLORIA KNIGHT

A PORCH IS

AN OUTSIDE EXTENSION

OF THE LOVE

THAT'S FOUND INSIDE.

A porch is

a place you come home to. . .

a place you retreat to. . .

a place you come back to

over and over again.

A house becomes a home

when each room is clothed with peace,

each wall is covered with laughter,

and each heart is filled with love.

A FRONT PORCH IS
LIKE A WELCOME SMILE
WHEN YOU ARRIVE HOME;
A FIREPLACE IS
LIKE A WARM HELLO
WHEN YOU STEP INSIDE.

*P*orches warm us from the inside out.

When you're relaxing on a front porch,

you don't have to worry about

getting up and adjusting the thermostat.

*A house will
always seem warm if
it has lots of pillows inside
and a cozy porch outside.*

*T*he crown of the home is godliness;

The beauty of the home is order;

The glory of the home is hospitality;

The blessing of the home is contentment.

HENRY VAN DYKE

How precious is

your unfailing love, O God!

All humanity finds shelter

in the shadow of your wings.

You feed them from the

abundance of your own house,

letting them drink from

your rivers of delight.

PSALM 36:7–8 NLT

One nice thing

about a front porch

that's being used is

that you don't have to knock

on the door to find out

if anyone is at home.

Snapshots from a Front Porch

Babies being rocked to sleep on the porch glider. . . warm blankets to snuggle up in. . .courting your sweetheart. . .teary-eyed welcomes and tear-filled good-byes. . .conversations that last long into the night. . .relaxing breaks from busy household chores. . .kids afoot. . .the dog by the steps. . .dirty boots by the side of the screen door. . .the comforting sound of family laughter. . . singing songs with a guitar accompaniment. . . carrying out cold leftovers by the armful. . .the beauty of being together.

WHEN A PORCH HAS BEEN

AROUND A LONG TIME,

IT'S NOT OLD,

IT'S "SEASONED."

Front Porch Vocabulary

welcoming, inviting, freeing—

delighting, invigorating, refreshing—

covering, protecting, shielding—

uniting, warming, inspiring—

rocking, swinging, playing—

informing, visiting, chatting—

napping, stretching, relaxing

The porch is a place we build with our hands and
maintain with our hearts.

———————

"I like to wait for Grandpa
to come home so that we can
go out on the porch
and build blocks together."

GRACE NAST, AGE 4

What a Treat

Grandma and I had a front porch summer tradition. I would take a seat on her porch cot with the squeaky springs and soft flannel blanket while she prepared one of my favorite things of all, a root-beer float. When she was finished, she would come join me on the cot where we would sit, and talk, and laugh, and slurp floats together. What a treat it was to not only have root-beer floats, but to have Grandma by my side.

$\mathcal{B}$egin a day with breakfast on the porch.
Start with waffles, real butter and warm syrup,
add some bacon and cold juice, and top it off with
hot coffee or hot apple cider.

These cornmeal and oat bran waffles are
flavorful and healthy. They take a bit of extra
time to make, but the results are always worth it.

Cornmeal and Oat Bran Waffles

1 cup flour

½ cup oat bran

½ cup cornmeal

2 tablespoons sugar

¼ cup almonds, chopped

2 teaspoons baking powder

½ teaspoon baking soda

¾ teaspoon salt

2 eggs, separated

2 cups buttermilk

¼ cup butter, melted

Preheat waffle iron. Combine dry ingredients in large bowl. Beat egg yolks. Beat in buttermilk and butter. Stir in dry ingredients until moist. In separate bowl, beat egg whites until stiff but not dry. Fold into batter. Bake on waffle iron and enjoy this unique, crunchy, flavorful waffle.

"Here I am!

I stand at the door and knock.

If anyone hears my voice and opens the door,

I will come in and eat with him,

and he with me."

REVELATION 3:20 NIV

The best thing

that can happen

to a porch is

wearing out from

too much use!

A Prayer for Our Home

Lord, may Your presence surround our borders,

Your grace cover our dwelling, Your truth
secure our foundation,

Your wisdom guard our gates, Your light
shine through our windows,

Your peace fill our rooms, Your joy echo
through our hallways, and

Your love indwell our hearts.

Porch Fun

One extremely hot and humid summer day during the Depression years, we were sitting on our front porch enjoying a delicious, cold, ripe watermelon. Times were tough, but laughter was a way of life with my mother, Emma. My dad, Jonas, was a bit more serious. As my sister and I watched Daddy savor the flavor of his juicy piece of melon, we were not prepared for what followed. To our great surprise, Mom and Daddy started shooting watermelon seeds at each other! The last shot taken by Mom hit Daddy right in the eye! We laughed so hard that we cried. That laugh is still in my heart today.

HANNAH KENNEDY

A cheerful heart

is good medicine.

PROVERBS 17:22 NLT

Everyone's favorite—these floats taste even better being sipped while sitting on a screened-in porch with glasses that are filled to the top with homemade ice cream.

Grandma's Root-Beer Floats

Frosted glasses or mugs

Root beer

Vanilla ice cream

Place glass or mug in freezer for 10 minutes prior to serving; remove from freezer. Pour root beer into container until half full. Now scoop ice cream in slowly. By putting root beer in first, the float does not foam. Enjoy this timeless treat!

HAVING A COZY
FRONT PORCH IS LIKE
GETTING A WARM HUG
EACH TIME YOU
STEP OUTSIDE.

A Garden View

Our hearts are God's garden;

His words are the seeds,

His grace brings the water;

His love pulls the weeds.

His hand does the pruning;

His truth is the hoe.

His caring presence

makes every—

thing grow.

The home improves happiness

and abates misery by

doubling our joy

and dividing our grief.

JOSEPH ADDISON

It is from God's heart that

the true values of

a home are established,

for no one values

an individual life,

or a family,

more than God.

The Blessings a Home Can Provide

How blessed are the children who grow up in a loving home and know the security of being cared for and valued;

Who enjoy the adventures of childhood while having wise guidance in discovering God's purpose for their lives;

Who have modeled before them the loving care of their heavenly Father, and who receive the benefits of faithful prayers.

Pay close attention, friend,

to what your father tells you;

never forget what you learned

at your mother's knee.

Wear their counsel like flowers in your hair,

like rings on your fingers.

PROVERBS 1:8–9 MSG

ONE OF THE STRONGEST
FORTIFICATIONS WHICH
THE HUMAN HEART CAN
THROW UP AGAINST TEMPTATION
IS THE HOME.

JOHN MCGOVERN

Prayer for the Day

Lord, guide my steps as I start this day;

Walk with me through the sunshine or rain;

When the night's shadows begin to fall,

Please bring me safely home again.

Jesus Is. . .

the baker's Bread,

the quilter's Pattern,

the homemaker's Guest,

the gardener's Rose,

the writer's Story,

the musician's Song,

the heart's Delight.

God,

bless our home with peace—

for it is as we yield

to Your control

that we find our rest.

God, fill our home with love—

for it is as we let Your heart

touch ours that we seek

the highest good of others.

God, fill our home with happiness—

for it is as we follow Your will

that we find the center of all joy.

FOR THE LORD
WATCHES OVER
THE WAY OF
THE RIGHTEOUS.

PSALM 1:6 NIV

When God watches over our lives, it is not in the same way someone watches TV or a movie. God is not a casual observer who passively sits back and watches the action take place around Him. When God watches over us, it is as a mother who watches over her young— knowing where the child is at all times, providing the things the child needs, sheltering the child from danger, and protecting the child from harm. God not only sees what is happening to us, He also understands why it is happening and knows how to handle it.

*A*re you not surprised to find how independent of money peace of conscience is and how much happiness can be condensed in the humblest home? A cottage will not hold the bulky furniture and sumptuous accommodations of a mansion; but if God be there, a cottage will hold as much happiness as might stock a palace.

DR. JAMES HAMILTON

Extol the LORD, O Jerusalem;

praise your God, O Zion,

for he strengthens the bars of your gates

and blesses your people within you.

He grants peace to your borders

and satisfies you with the finest of wheat.

PSALM 147:12–14 NIV

I call to remembrance

the genuine faith that is in you,

which dwelt first in your grandmother Lois

and your mother Eunice,

and I am persuaded is in you also.

2 TIMOTHY 1:5 NKJV

A genuine faith is like a golden thread that joins the hearts of one generation to the hearts of another.

To understand the heart of God is to understand the heart of the home. He is the Father from whom the whole family in heaven and earth is named. From His heart flows everything that means family. He is the first to love, to care, to nurture, to comfort, to cherish, to instruct, to train, to heal, and to provide. He is the One who shelters and covers us with His wings. He is the One who has given the family its order, its foundation, its values, and its worth. He is the One who has called it into being, sanctified it, hallowed it, and honored it with His blessing.

HOME IS
WHERE THE STRONG CORDS
OF COMMITMENT BIND
HEARTS TOGETHER WITH
THE CLOSEST TIES OF LOVE.

Home is in the people,
Its atmosphere and grace;
With all its charm and beauty,
Home is a special place.
Home is where we gather
To meet each other's needs;
Home is felt within the heart
In thoughts, in words, in deeds.

It has been said that the sweetest words in our language are "mother," "home," and "heaven"; and one might almost say the word "home" included them all; for who can think of home without remembering the gentle mother who sanctified it by her presence? And is not home the dearest name for heaven? We think of that better land as a home where brightness will never end in night.

Oh, then, may our homes on earth be the centers of all our joys; may they be as green spots in the desert, to which we can retire when weary of the cares and perplexities of life, and drink the clear waters of a love, which we know to be sincere and always unfailing.

extracted from *SATURDAY EVENING POST,*
late 1800s issue

The memory of the beautiful
and happy home of childhood is
the richest legacy any mother and father
can leave to their children.

B. G. NORTHRUP

Home is a place where the nightlight is always on, where the welcome mat is always out, and where the door is always open.

THERE IS NO VELVET SO SOFT AS

a mother's lap. . .

NO ROSE SO SWEET AS

a mother's cheek. . .

NO MUSIC SO CHARMING AS

a mother's voice.

BISHOP NEWMAN

Words We Love to Hear

"Please come in."

"Time to eat."

"I'll be praying for you."

"It's so good to see you."

"I've been thinking about you."

"Can you stay?"

"I've missed you."

"Welcome home."

"Pull up a chair."

"Come sit awhile."

*L*ove GOD, your God, with your whole
heart: love him with all that's in you, love him
with all you've got! Write these commandments
that I've given you today on your hearts. Get
them inside of you and then get them inside
your children. Talk about them wherever you
are, sitting at home or walking in the street;
talk about them from the time you get up in the
morning to when you fall into bed at night. Tie
them on your hands and foreheads as a reminder;
inscribe them on the doorposts of your homes
and on your city gates.

DEUTERONOMY 6:5–9 MSG

The godly home is an informal university with classes that are conducted seven days a week. It has the most caring and qualified teachers, who know the hearts of their students better than anyone else. The curriculum covers every subject that pertains to life and its meaning—including the development of character, the establishment of faith, the value of relationships, and the meaning of love.

*H*ome and family can bring us

incredible wealth.

Who can be richer than

those who have shared joy-filled

times, who have known the gifts

of love and companionship,

and who carry within them

a treasure chest filled with

cherished memories.

Home Is Where. . .

hearts are united

hands are joined

characters are formed

truth is spoken

values are established

care is given

love serves all

For this cause I bow my knees

unto the Father of our Lord Jesus Christ,

Of whom the whole family

in heaven and earth is named.

EPHESIANS 3:14–15 KJV

he more we learn about God as our
Father, the more we understand the meaning of a
family. Through the love a man shows to his
wife, through the submission that a woman gives
to her husband, and through the honor that chil-
dren give to their parents, the image of God is
reflected in a home.

here is a harvest of blessings to be reaped from a home that is planted in the soil of God's love—guidance and instruction, nurturing and care, wisdom and concern, shelter and provisions, help and support, affirmation and identity, security and protection.

A parent,

whose trust is in the Lord,

can make an eternal difference

in the life of a child.

The little girl's eyes opened wide when she
saw Grandma sitting on the front-porch swing.
She ran into her grandma's arms and beamed
with a broad smile when Grandma lifted her
up and placed the little girl in her lap. To the
little girl, Grandma's arms were a special
hugging place, and Grandma's lap was a favorite
snuggling place.

A mother is a collection of good things—

A caring smile, a giving way,

A servant's heart day after day;

A ceaseless love, a tender touch,

A thousand joys that mean so much.

A kitchen is a special place—

where people gather,

where bread is broken,

where hearts freely share,

where caring hands serve.

Blest be the tie that binds

our hearts in Christian love;

The fellowship of kindred minds

is like to that above.

Before our Father's throne

we pour our ardent prayers;

Our fears, our hopes, our aims are one,

our comforts and our cares.

JOHN FAWCETT

The generous prosper and are satisfied;

those who refresh others

will themselves be refreshed.

PROVERBS 11:25 NLT

Lord, thank You for the resources we have been

given within our home to extend blessings to

others. Fill our hearts with Your

compassion, and use our

hands as instruments

of Your love.

Memories of Three Porches

I wish every little girl could grow up with a porch or two in her memory. I remember three—the screened-in back porch where my sister and I took our baths in a big metal tub, the high front porch where we greeted visitors and friends, and the front porch at Grandma and Grandpa's house just over the meadow. It was at Grandma and Grandpa's house that my heart gathered a treasure of memories. What a joy it was taking naps on the front porch swing as Grandma gently pushed it, delighting in the sights and smells of the cornfield that stood nearby, and crunching on the freshly cut apples that had been picked by my grandpa and sliced to perfection with his special pocketknife.

BETTY WOMACK

ord, may each person who enters our home be greeted with a smile, welcomed with delight, treated with honor, served with humility, and cared for in the same way that we would treat You if You were our guest.

WE NEED NOT POWER

NOR SPLENDOR,

WIDE HALL

NOR LORDLY DOME;

THE GOOD, THE TRUE,

THE TENDER—

THESE FORM THE

WEALTH OF HOME.

AUTHOR UNKNOWN

*The first thing
that God did after He
created man and woman
was to establish the home.*

BILLY GRAHAM

THE FRONT PORCH IS
A GREAT PLACE FOR
A FAMILY GETAWAY—
CLOSE BY, INEXPENSIVE,
ACCOMMODATING,
AND UTTERLY DELIGHTFUL.

*A*s for me and my house,

we will serve the LORD.

JOSHUA 24:15 KJV